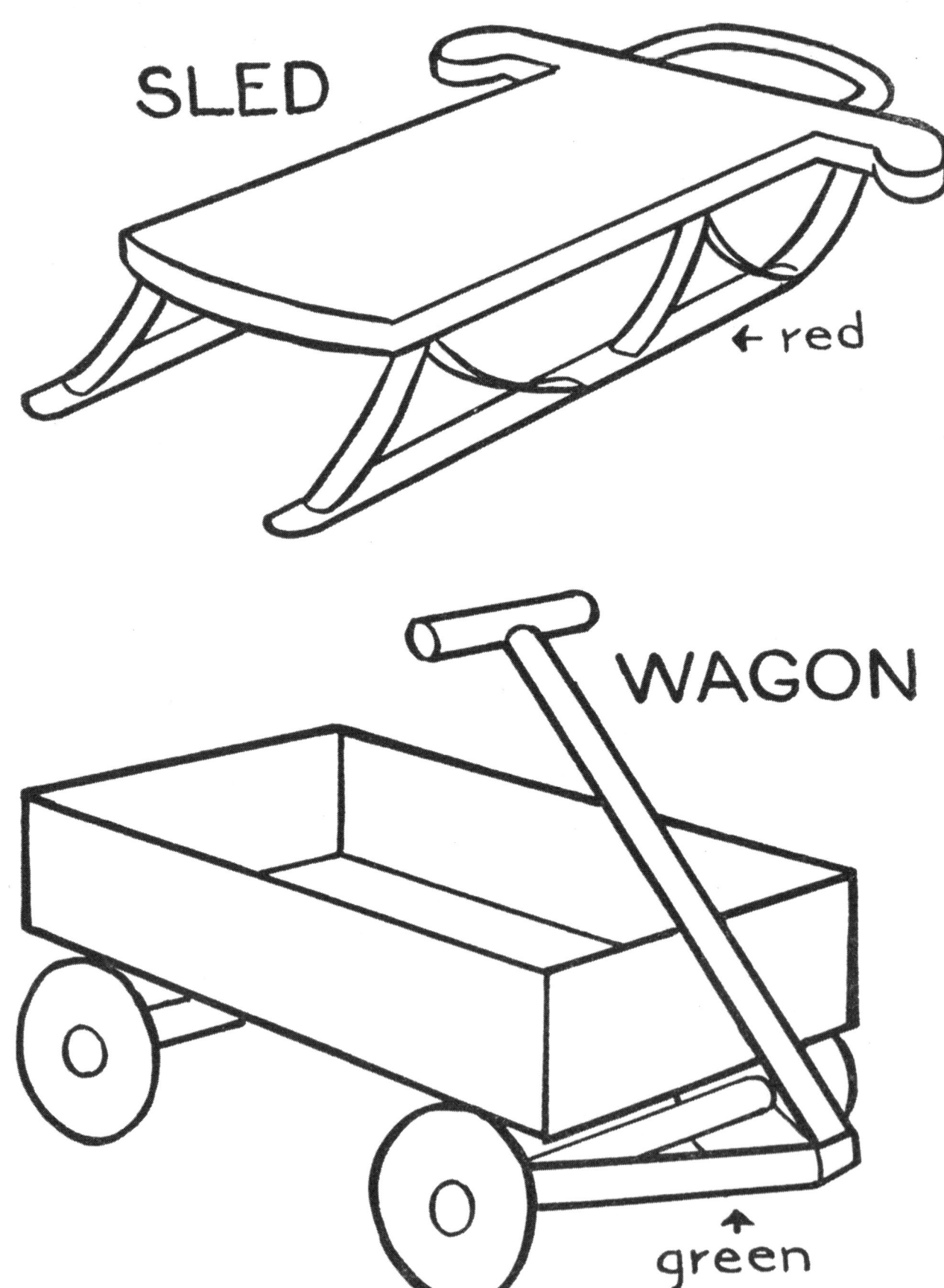

Published by Paper Studio Press, P.O. Box 14, Kingfield, ME 04947, 800-290-2928, paperstudiopress.com
This is a reproduction of In The Candy Cane House Easy Coloring, No. 4890, originally published by Merrill Co. Publishers in 1955.
ISBN: 978-1-935223-83-2

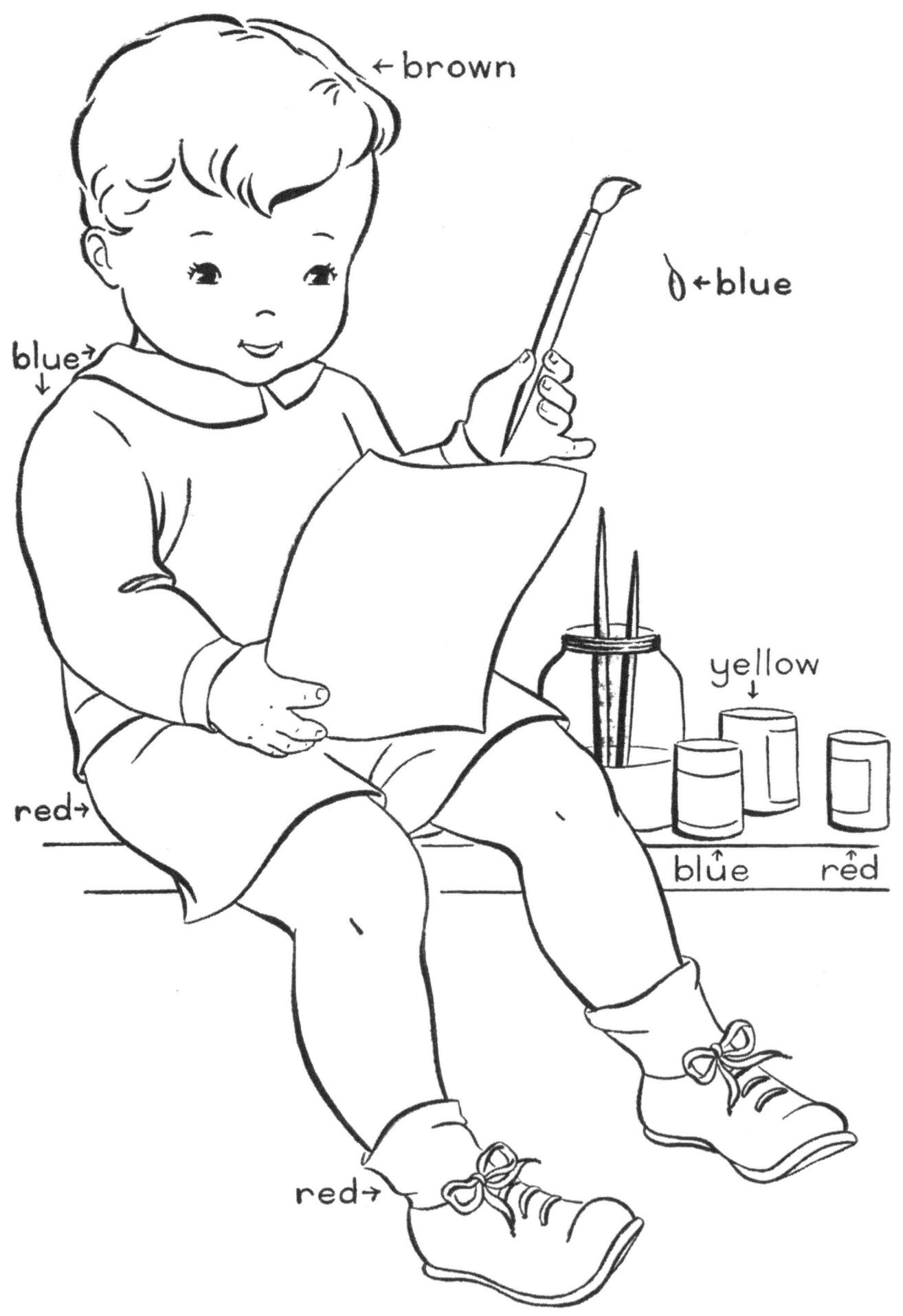

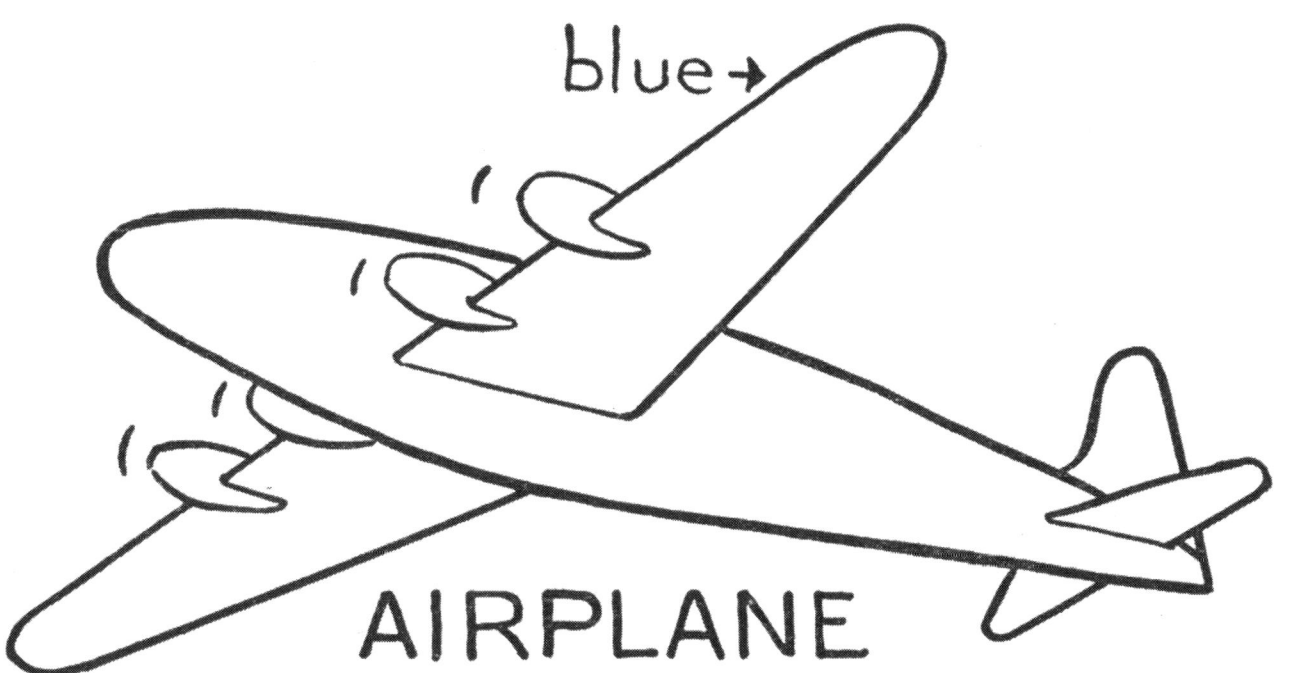

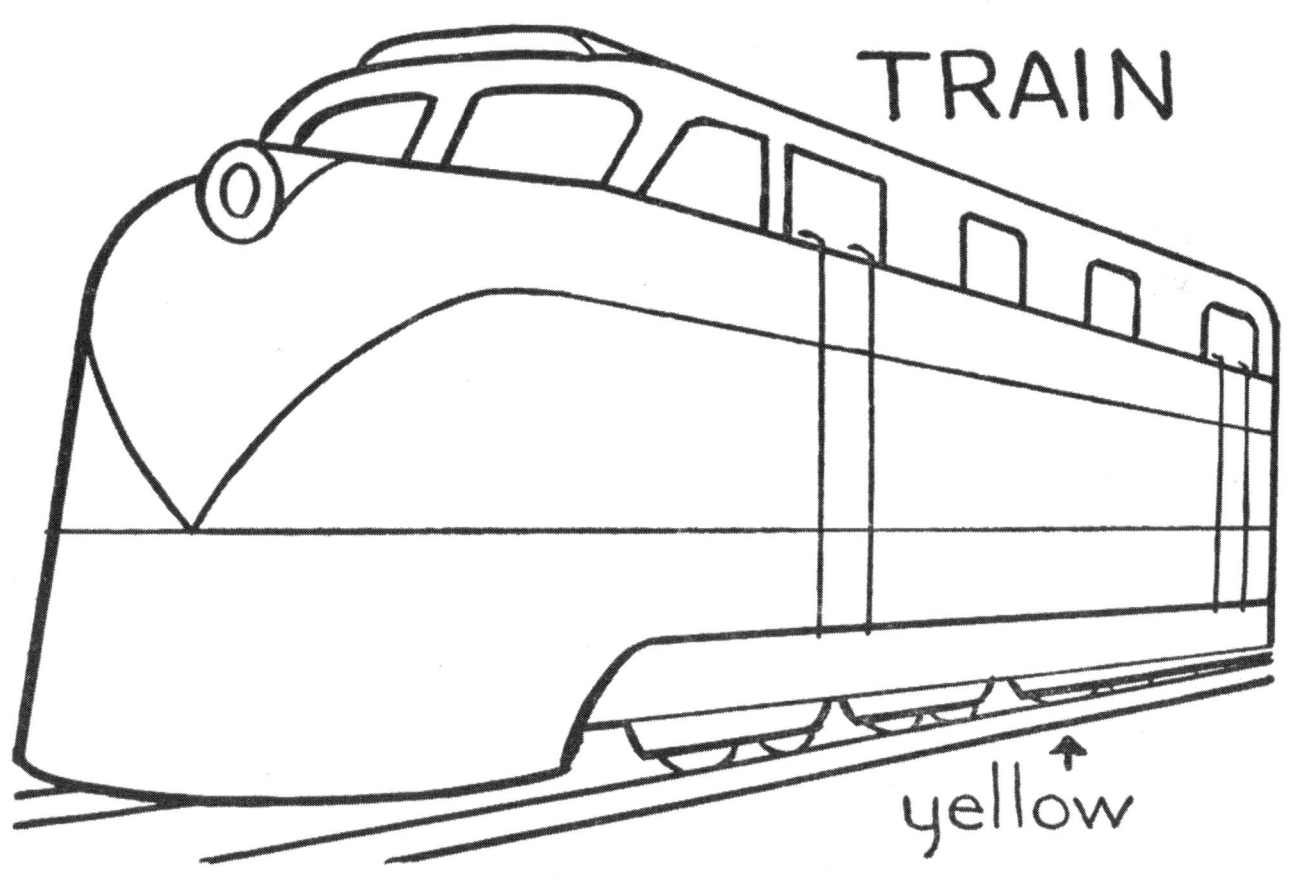

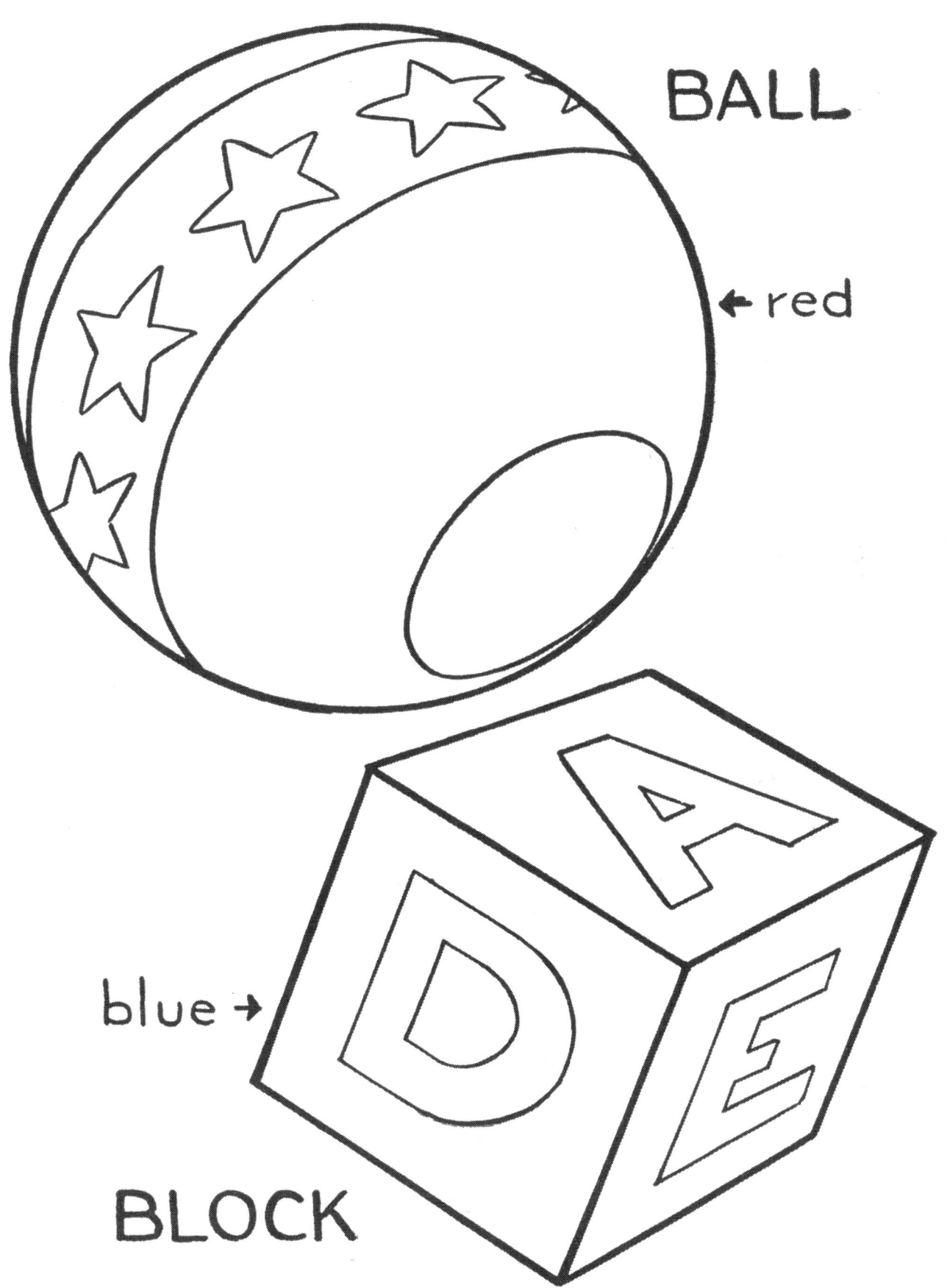

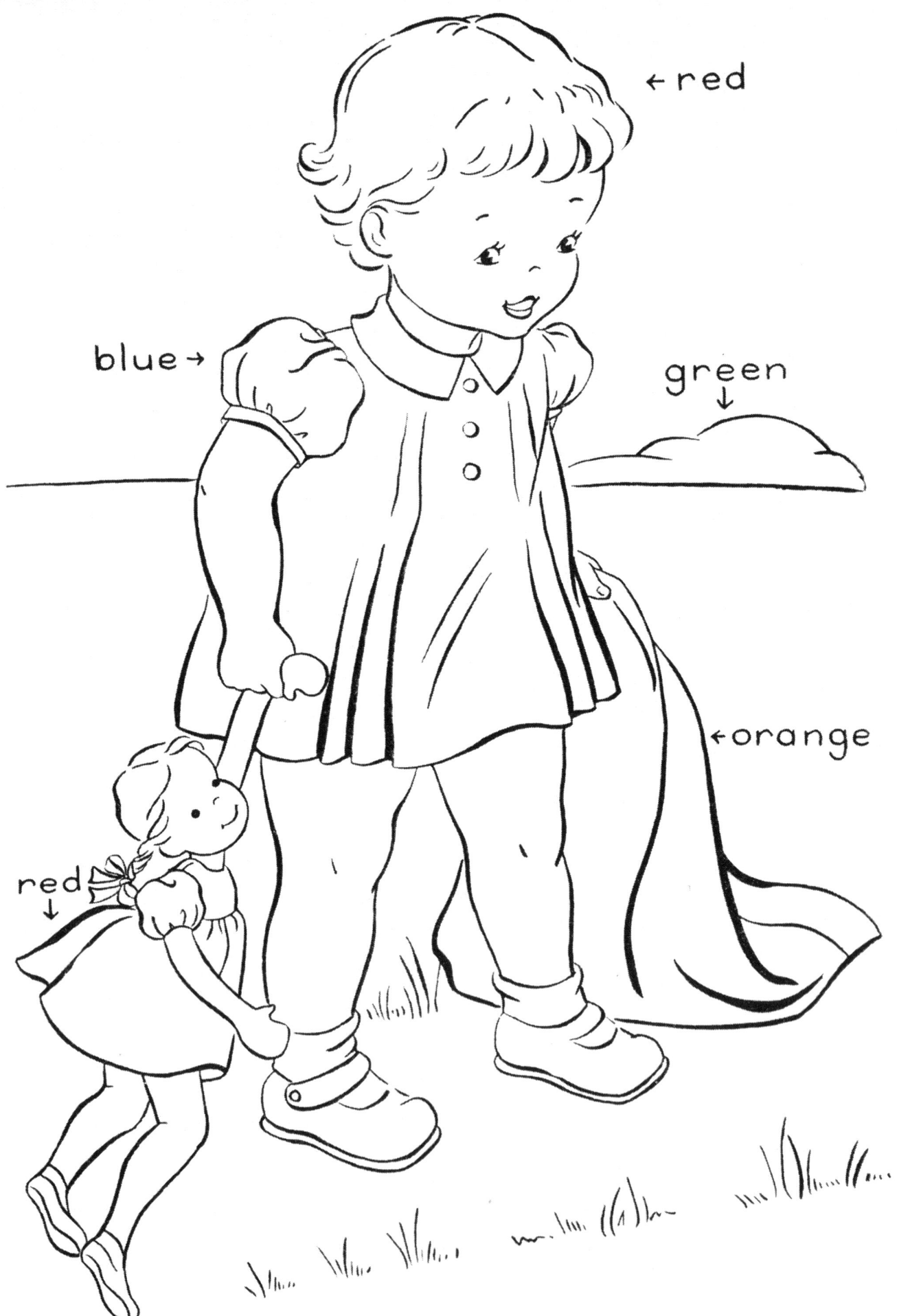

EASY TO COLOR

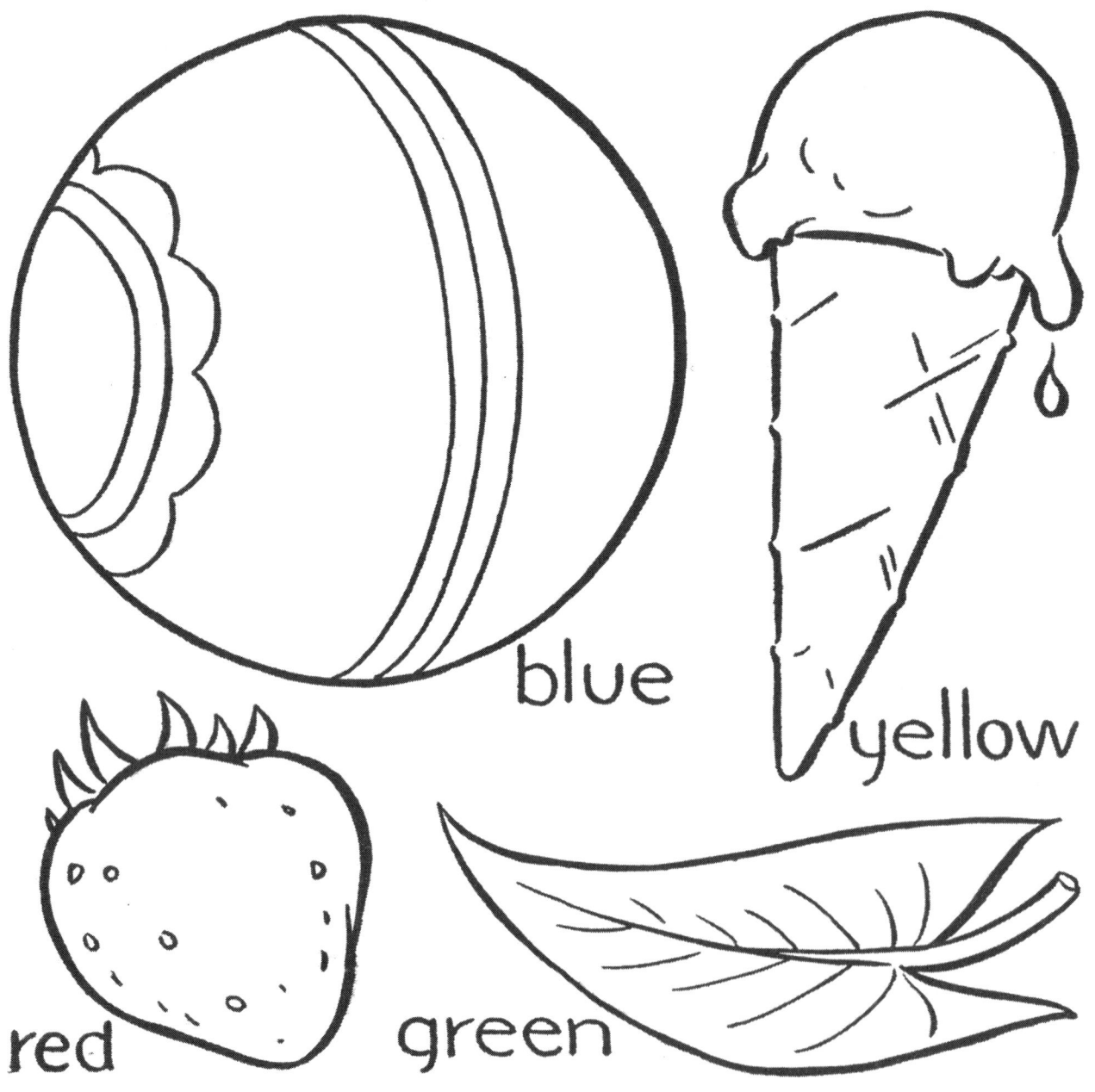

blue

yellow

red

green

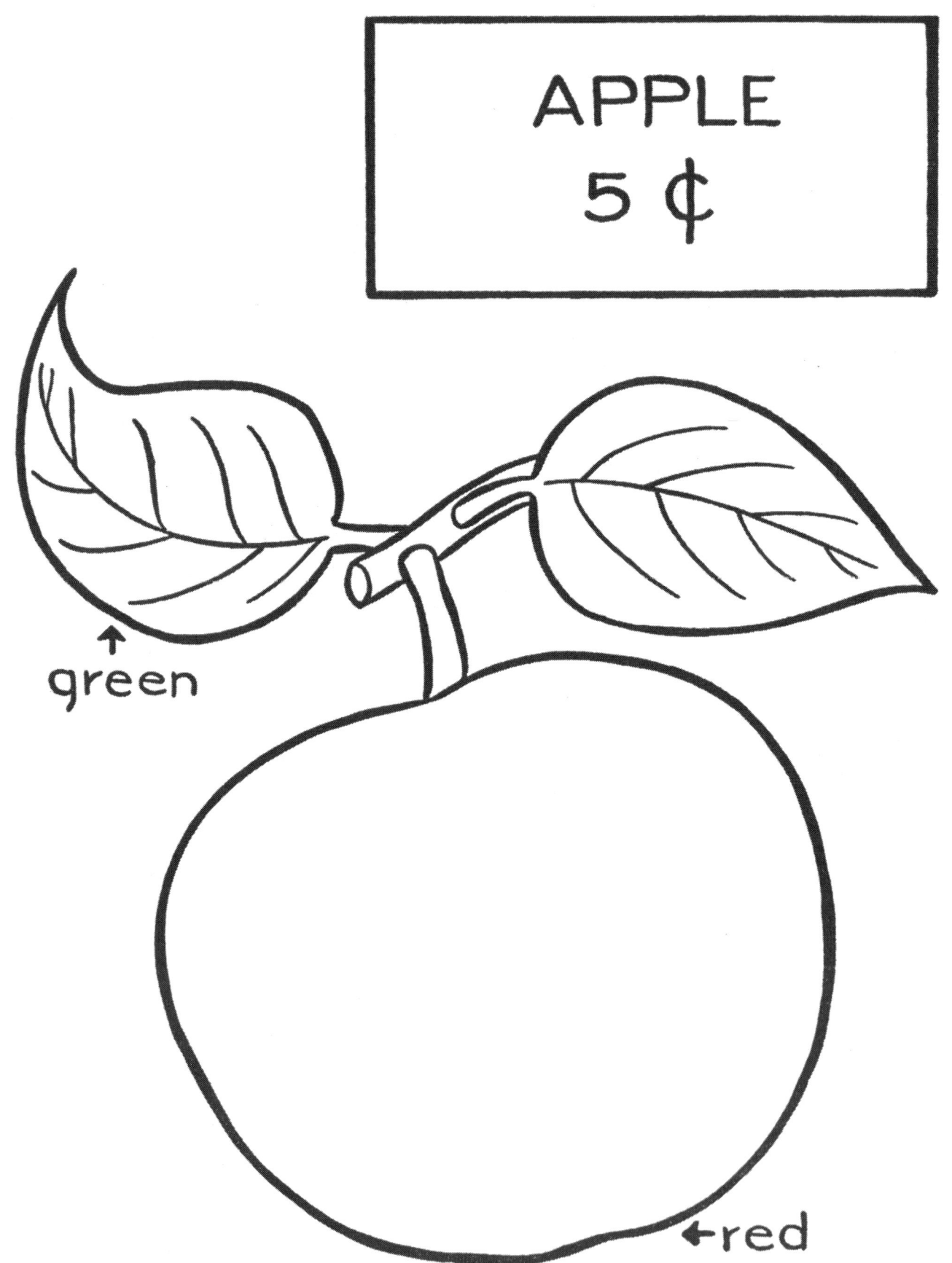

STRAWBERRY

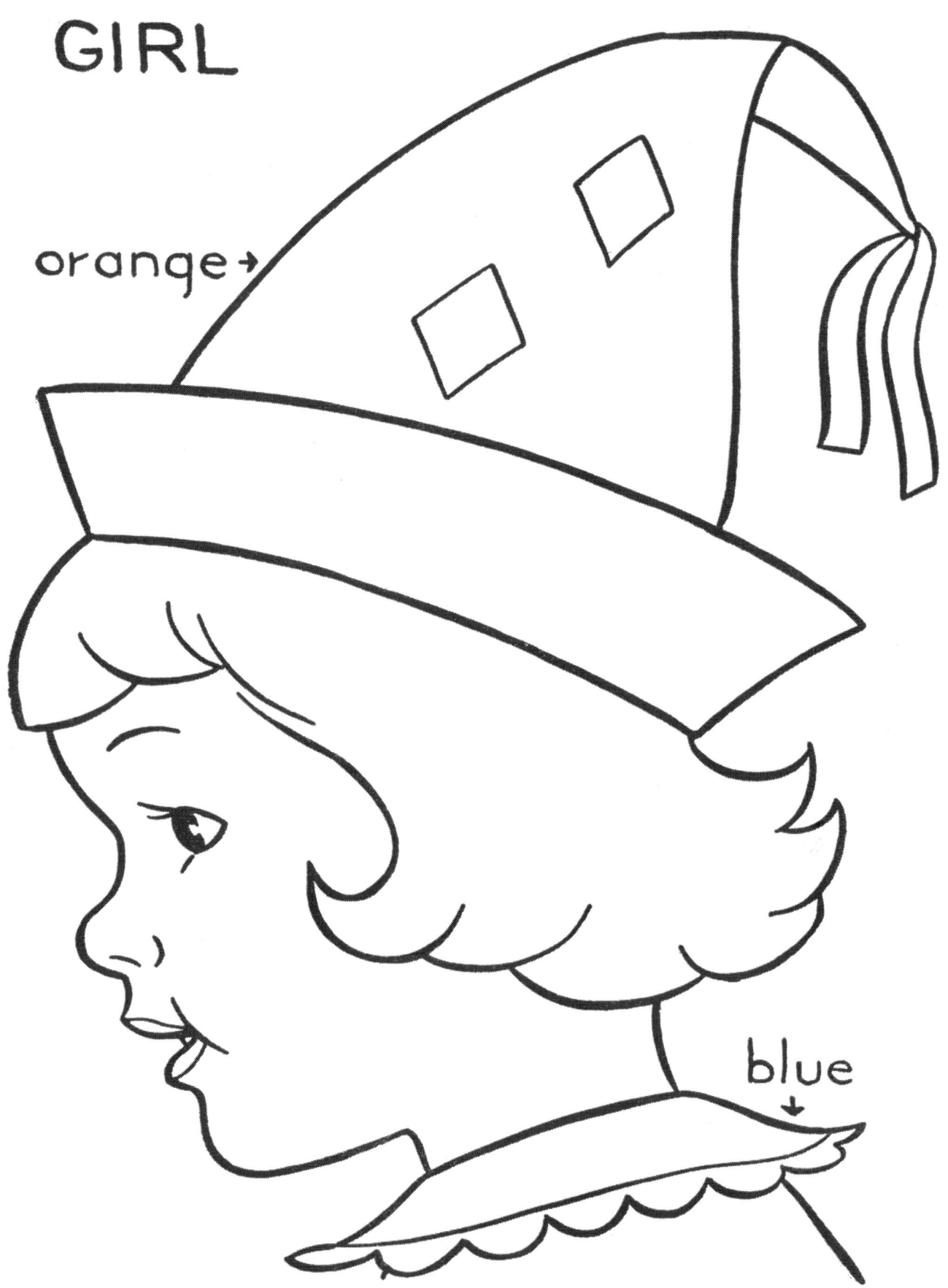

GIRL

← orange

blue →

Made in the USA
San Bernardino, CA
20 March 2016